Helping Children See Jesus

ISBN: 978-1-64104-031-0

Godly/Ungodly Living
Old Testament Volume 26:
Kings, Chronicles, Minor Prophets Part 4

Authors: Katherine E. Hershey (Kings/Chronicles);
Gertrude Landis (Minor Prophets)
Illustrator: Vernon Henkel
Computer Graphic Artists: Olivia and Bethany Moy
Page Layout: Patricia Pope

© 2022 Bible Visuals International
PO Box 153, Akron, PA 17501-0153
Phone: (717) 859-1131
www.biblevisuals.org

All rights reserved. No part of this publication may be reproduced, stored in a retrieval system or transmitted in any form by any means, electronic, mechanical, photocopy, recording or otherwise, without the prior permission of the publisher, except as provided by USA copyright law.

RELATED ITEMS

To access related items (such as activities, memory verse posters and translated texts) please visit our web store at www.biblevisuals.org and enter 2026 at the top right of the web page. You may need to reduce the zoom setting to get the search box.

FREE TEXT DOWNLOAD

To obtain a FREE printable copy of the English teaching text (PDF format) under Product Format, please scroll down and select Extra–PDF Teacher Text Download. Then under Language select English before clicking the ADD TO CART button to place in your shopping cart. Other languages are available at an additional cost from the Language menu. When checking out, use coupon code XTACSV17 at checkout and click on Apply Coupon to receive the discount on the English text.

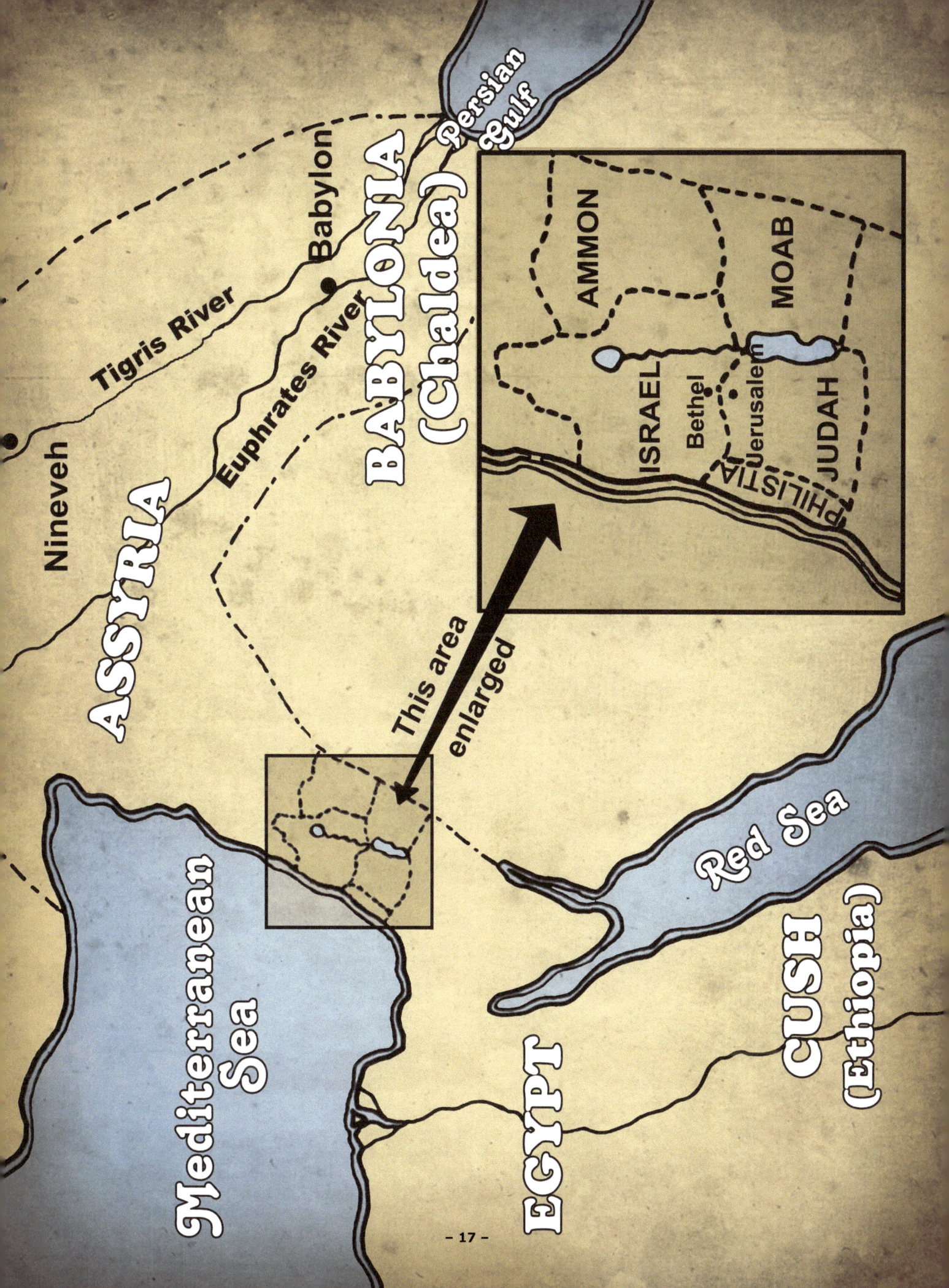

If My people, which are called by My name, shall humble themselves, and pray, and seek My face, and turn from their wicked ways, then will I hear from Heaven, and will forgive their sin, and will heal their land.

2 Chronicles 7:14

Lesson 1
GOD HEARS PRAYER

NOTE TO THE TEACHER

Have you used Volume 11 (Leviticus, Part 1) of this series? If so, your students will be familiar with the three offerings mentioned in this lesson. This would be a good time to review the meaning of these offerings.

1. *Sin offering* (See 2 Chronicles 29:21; Leviticus 4:3). A required offering, given as a sacrifice for sin. The sinner acknowledged his guilt. The innocent animal died in the sinner's place.
2. *Burnt offering* (see 2 Chronicles 29:24, 27; Leviticus 1:3-4). A voluntary offering given to God. It was the person's way of saying, "I am willingly setting myself apart for God."
3. *Thank offering* (also called *Fellowship [Peace] offering*, see 2 Chronicles 29:31; Leviticus 3:1; 7:11-21). This happy offering was a gift of thanks to God.

You may want to divide each of these lesson in half. Therefore we have suggested a closing paragraph after the second point of each lesson. An opening for the second half of the lesson is also included.

Begin each lesson with a brief review asking questions. Your students will remember what they have opportunity to tell.

When we first began our study, Israel was a great nation. Solomon was the wise king. HE built a magnificent temple where the people of God could worship Him. God said, "My house will be holy. I shall put My name there forever. My eyes and My heart shall always be there" (1 Kings 9:3). Jerusalem was the capital of all Israel. It became a great city because God's wonderful temple was there.

After King Solomon died, the nation was torn apart. The Southern Kingdom was named for its larger tribe, Judah. The Northern Kingdom kept the name Israel. For more than 200 years, wicked kings led the Northern Kingdom away from God. So Israel had become a weak nation. Finally it was invaded by Assyria, a strong, wicked nation. The people of Israel were captured because "they neither listened to God's commands nor obeyed them." (See 2 Kings 18:11-12.) So the Israelites, God's people, were swept away into foreign lands. There they lived among God's enemies. This was the end of the large Northern Kingdom. Our lesson today begins seven years later in the Southern Kingdom, Judah.

Scripture to be studied: 2 Kings 18:1-19:37; 2 Chronicles 29:1-32:33; Isaiah 36:1-37:38

The *aim* of the lesson: To teach that God hears the prayers of His own and answers according to His will.

What your students should *know*: All sin must be confessed to God in prayer.

What your students should *feel*: Eager to pray to the Lord about everything.

What your students should *do*: Set aside a definite time for daily prayer.

Lesson outline (for the teacher's and students' notebooks):

1. Hezekiah's prayer of worship (2 Chronicles 29:20-36).
2. Hezekiah's prayer for forgiveness (2 Chronicles 30:1-31:21).
3. Hezekiah's prayer for help (2 Chronicles 32:1-20; 2 Kings 18:13-17; 19:1-34; Isaiah 36:1-2, 13-22; 37:1-13, 21-25).
4. Hezekiah's prayer is answered (2 Chronicles 32:21-23; 2 Kings 19:35-37; Isaiah 37:36-38).

The verse to be memorized:

If My people, which are called by My name, shall humble themselves, and pray, and seek My face, and turn from their wicked ways, then will I hear from Heaven, and will forgive their sin, and will heal their land.

(2 Chronicles 7:14)

THE LESSON

Judah, the Southern Kingdom, now had a good king, Hezekiah. (See 2 Chronicles 29:1-2.) Hezekiah's wicked father (King Ahaz) had turned the people away from God. So good King Hezekiah called together the priests and Levites. These were men who helped God's people to worship Him.

"Listen!" King Hezekiah commanded his men. "Set yourselves apart. And set apart the temple for the Lord God. Clean out God's temple. Our fathers were wicked (sinful and ungodly). They turned their backs on God. They stopped worshiping Him. They shut the temple doors. (See 2 Chronicles 29:3-11.) God is angry about this. (See 2 Chronicles 28:22-25.) I am now promising God we shall change. If we do right, God will no longer be angry with us. Now get to work!"

Immediately the men started working. For 16 days they cleaned the inside and outside of God's magnificent temple. Then they reported to King Hezekiah: "The work is finished. The filth is gone. Everything has been cleaned. The temple is now ready for worship." (See 2 Chronicles 29:12-19.)

1. HEZEKIAH'S PRAYER OF WORSHIP
2 Chronicles 29:20-36

Early the next morning, King Hezekiah called the city officials. Together they went up to God's temple, taking along 28 animals. These were *sin offerings*. They were sacrificed to God for the sins of all Israel–and for the temple. King Hezekiah commanded, "Now place the *burnt offerings* on the altar." The people willingly offered their sacrifices. By doing this, each was saying, "I am setting myself apart for God." Immediately the musicians began playing their instruments. And the singers sang. Oh. how they sang! It was a happy time. The temple was clean. And the people were now forgiven of their sin.

Show Illustration #1

So the king and all the people bowed to worship God. What did they say when they worshiped Him? We do not know. To worship God is to speak of His great worth. God had forgiven them. So they may have told Him: "You, Lord, are

– 19 –

worthy of honor and praise." (See, for example, Revelation 4:11; 5:12.)

Then King Hezekiah told the Levites, "Sing praise to the Lord." This they did gladly. Afterward they bowed their heads and again worshiped God.

King Hezekiah turned to all the people. "You have set yourselves apart for the Lord," he said. "Now bring your sacrifices and *thank offerings* to Him." With "willing hearts" the people brought almost 4,000 animals. Some gave *burnt offerings*. These were gifts of love to God. Others brought *thank offerings*. They were thanking God for forgiving their sins and giving them peace.

So the service of the temple was set in order. And King Hezekiah and the people were happy because God's temple had been cleaned quickly. (See 2 Chronicles 29:36.)

God heard the worship of King Hezekiah, the Levites, and the people. And He hears you when you worship Him.

2. HEZEKIAH'S PRAYER FOR FORGIVENESS
2 Chronicles 30:1-31:21

King Hezekiah wanted all the people in the land to celebrate Passover. This was a most important, solemn ceremony for God's people. (See Exodus 12 and Numbers 9:1-14.) Passover was to be observed every year. So King Hezekiah sent his messengers to everyone in Judah (the Southern Kingdom). They even went to those in Israel who had escaped Assyrian capture.

The messengers read King Hezekiah's invitation. It said: "Come to the temple in Jerusalem for Passover." To those in the Northern Kingdom, Israel, the king added, "You people in Israel who have escaped from the king of Assyria, turn again to the Lord God. Then He will return to you. Yield yourselves to the Lord. Come to His temple. Serve the Lord your God so He will no longer be angry with you. The Lord is good and kind." Most of the people of Israel laughed at the messengers. They worshiped their calf idols! Only a few humbled themselves and accepted the king's invitation.

But the people of Judah really wanted to celebrate Passover. (See 2 Chronicles 30:12.) So a large crowd streamed into Jerusalem. They were surprised to see idols and incense altars there. So they tore them down at once and destroyed them. Earlier the temple had been cleaned. Now the city was also clean.

The people were really eager to observe Passover. So the priests and Levites killed the Passover lambs.

Show Illustration #2

Quickly King Hezekiah spoke to God for the people of Israel. He prayed, "May the Lord, who is good, forgive all who are truly seeking God." Hezekiah confessed that they had sinned and needed God's forgiveness. The Lord heard Hezekiah's prayer and answered it. He forgave the people and healed (did not punish) them. (See 2 Chronicles 30:18-20.) Together let's read our verse (2 Chronicles 7:14). (Draw attention to the word "heal.")

The celebration went on for days and days. Everyone was happy and thankful to God. The Levites and priests sang and played instruments the whole time. (See 2 Chronicles 30:21.) There had not been such a wonderful celebration for many years (not since the time of Solomon). (See 2 Chronicles 30:26.) "Then the priests and Levites blessed the people. And the Lord heard their prayers in His holy dwelling place, Heaven" (2 Chronicles 30:27).

Leaving the temple, the people of Israel went throughout all Judah and Israel. Everywhere they broke down the idols and heathen altars, destroying every one. Because they had truly turned to God, they were doing what pleased Him. And pleasing God is Godly living. Are you living to please God?

King Hezekiah reminded the people in Jerusalem to give offerings to the Lord. These would be used for the work of the priests in God's temple. The people promptly obeyed. They brought so much that rooms had to be built to store everything! (See 2 Chronicles 31:11.)

Good King Hezekiah did for the Lord what was right. And he did it with all his heart. So God made him successful. (See 2 Chronicles 31:20-21.) Hezekiah was living a Godly life. Are you? Hezekiah was a man who prayed about everything. Do you? Perhaps you wonder how to pray.

Remember, King Hezekiah first *worshiped God*. He then asked God's forgiveness for sin, which he would have *confessed*. Then God heard *thanksgiving* for what He had done for His people. In the next part of our lesson, we shall see that prayer also includes *asking God* for our needs.

Let's make a list of these in our notebooks.

PRAYER IS:
1. WORSHIPING GOD, telling Him how worthy He is of our praise.
2. CONFESSING SIN, naming each sin and asking God's forgiveness.
3. THANKING GOD for everything He does for us.
4. ASKING GOD for our needs.

3. HEZEKIAH'S PRAYER FOR HELP
2 Chronicles 32:1-20; 2 Kings 18:13-37; 19:1-34; Isaiah 36:1-2, 13-22; 37:1-13, 21-25

Hezekiah was a praying man. He *worshiped God* when he prayed. He *confessed his sin* and asked God's forgiveness. He joined the people in *thanking God* for what He had done. Surprisingly, even kings have needs. What do you suppose King Hezekiah needed? Listen carefully!

Assyria (show on map), the nation which had conquered Israel (the Northern Kingdom) years before, was getting stronger. Now the king of Assyria had plans to conquer Judah (the Southern Kingdom). So King Hezekiah paid a lot of silver and gold to the Assyrian king. (See 2 Kings 18:14-16.) He hoped this would keep Assyria away. But, no! The king of Assyria wanted more than silver and gold. He wanted cities–especially the city of Jerusalem. So his top officers led his great army to the Jerusalem city wall. (See 2 Kings 18:17; 2 Chronicles 32:1-5.)

King Hezekiah knew his people were afraid of the Assyrians. Lovingly he spoke to them, saying, "Be strong! Have courage! Do not be afraid of the king of Assyria or his huge army. We have the Lord our God with us. He will help us." The people trusted their king and were encouraged. (See 2 Chronicles 32:7-8.)

Later the Assyrian officers spoke to the people of Jerusalem. One proudly announced, "We have come from the great king of Assyria. This is what he says: 'On what are you trusting? Do you think Assyria cannot capture Jerusalem? Your king says the Lord your God will save you from us. But he is deceiving you. You know we Assyrians have conquered every nation we attacked. The gods of those nations could not save them. Nor can your God save you! Do not believe Hezekiah.'" (See 2 Kings 18:18-24; 2 Chronicles 32:9-16; Isaiah 36:13-21.)

This awful news had to be taken to King Hezekiah at once. Three men tore their clothes (showing their great sadness), and hurried to the king. When Hezekiah heard what the Assyrians had said, he also tore his clothes. Covering himself with rough cloth, he rushed to God's holy temple.

Show Illustration #3

There, King Hezekiah cried, praying to the Lord. (See 2 Kings 19:1; **Isaiah 37:1**.) Do you think He asked God for His protection? (Let students discuss.) Praying to God includes *asking for our needs*.

Coming from the temple, King Hezekiah gave orders to some of his men. "Go to **ISAIAH** the *prophet* of God. Tell him what the king of Assyria says."

The men, covered with rough clothing, hurried to **ISAIAH** with their bad news.

ISAIAH carefully listened to their problem. Soon he spoke God's message. "The Lord says, 'Tell your master Hezekiah not to be afraid. Tell him not to be worried by the words spoken against Me. I shall send trouble to the king of Assyria. He will return to his own land. There I shall cause him to die by the sword'." (Sec 2 Kings 19:6-7; Isaiah 37:6-7.)

The men rushed the good news to King Hezekiah.

In time, King Hezekiah received a letter from the Assyrian king. He read: "Do not let God, in whom you trust, deceive you. Do not believe God when He says, 'Jerusalem will not be captured by the king of Assyria.' You know Assyria has completely destroyed other nations. Did their gods help them?" *(NO! See 2 Kings 19:10-13; Isaiah 37:10-13.)*

Show Illustration #3

Hezekiah raced to the temple, taking the letter with him. There he laid it out as if asking, "Please, Lord, will You look at this?" Then Hezekiah prayed. "O Lord God, You alone are God. Please listen. Open your eyes, O Lord. O Lord our God, we plead with you to save us. Then the earth will know that You alone are God."

Shortly after his prayer, Hezekiah received an answer from God. It came through the **prophet ISAIAH**. God told Hezekiah what He would do to the Assyrian king. "I shall put My hook in his nose and My bridle in his mouth. I shall defend Jerusalem. I shall save it for My sake and for the sake of (King) David, My servant." (See 2 Kings 19:28-34; **Isaiah** 37:29-35.)

4. HEZEKIAH'S PRAYER IS ANSWERED
2 Chronicles 32:21-23; 2 Kings 19:35-37; Isaiah 37:36-38

That night, outside the walls of Jerusalem, there were 185,000 Assyrian soldiers. All were ready to destroy Jerusalem the next day.

Show Illustration #4

The Assyrian soldiers slept soundly that night. They had nothing to worry about. They were ready to wipe out Jerusalem. While they slept, an angel of the Lord went through their camp. And, when morning came, all 185,000 soldiers lay dead! The Assyrian army had been destroyed totally by the living God of Heaven. Shamefully, Assyrian's ungodly king went home to his capital city (Nineveh). There, while he worshiped his idols, his two sons stabbed him to death. (See 2 Kings 19:37.) **ISAIAH's** prophecy from God came true–every bit of it!

Who took care of King Hezekiah and the people of Jerusalem? The Lord Himself! Because Hezekiah prayed, God destroyed the entire Assyrian army.

King Hezekiah prayed about everything. Do you? He prayed at any time. Do you? Do you also have a particular time for prayer every day? If not, will you ask the Lord now to show you when you should have your prayer time? Will you promise God you will do your best to pray each day?

(*Teacher:* Allow time for silent prayer.)

Now let us have a time of prayer together. Who would like to *WORSHIP God*, telling Him how worthy He is of our praise? Who will lead us in *CONFESSING SINS* to the Lord? Which of you will *give THANKS to God* for something special He has done for you? Who will close, *ASKING God for some special need*?

Lesson 2
GOD HATES PRIDE

NOTE TO THE TEACHER

This series, contrasting Godly and ungodly living, touches on how Christians should and should not live. Before teaching today's lesson, carefully review lesson #1. Emphasize the absolute necessity of a good prayer life.

This lesson warns against pride, a sin God hates and punishes. (See Psalm 101:5; Proverbs 6:16-17; 16:5.) Pride is as old as Satan. He was created perfectly wise and beautiful. (See *Ezekiel* 28:12-17.) Then the sin of pride overcame him. (See 1 Timothy 3:6.) He wanted the glory which belonged to God alone. (Five times Satan said, "I will"–*Isaiah* 14;12-14.) So God cast Satan out of his original position in Heaven (*Ezekiel* 28:16). Ever since, Satan has continually set himself against God and God's people.

There are many sins with which Satan tempts Christian believers. The sin which caused good King Hezekiah's downfall, was pride. Because pride may seem quite harmless, we sometimes forget its awfulness. (But observe with what dreadful sins pride is included in Romans 1:29-31.) Pride is often the root of other sins. Spend time thinking fo the characteristic temptations of your students. You may discover that many sins are actually the fruit of pride.

Nineveh was the capital of Assyria, the first known empire in history. *JONAH* had prophesied to Nineveh. At that time, king and people repented and turned to God. Apparently they failed to lead their children to the Lord. So by the time of this lesson (125 years later), Assyrians were known for their terrible cruelty. They were guilty of cutting off people's hands, feet, ears, noses, heads. They gouged out eyes and skinned people alive. No wonder the prophet *NAHUM* spoke of Nineveh as "the bloody city." (See *Nahum* 3:1.)

When the Assyrians were cruel to God's people, God said they were raging against Him. (See 2 Kings 19:20-28.) For this, God said to the Assyrians, "I shall put My hook in your nose . . ." This was typical of the cruelties practiced by the Assyrians. What they had done to others, would be done to them.

All the prophecies of *ISAIAH* and *NAHUM* mentioned in this lesson came true long ago.

Scripture to be studied: 2 Kings 20:1-21:26; 2 Chronicles 32:24-33:25; Isaiah 38:1-8; 39:1-8; Nahum 1:1-3:9

The *aim* of the lesson: to teach God's hatred of pride and His readiness to forgive.

What your students should *know*: God hates pride.

What your students should *feel*: A desire to recognize pride and turn from it every day.

What your students should *do*: Confess all pride to God and ask His forgiveness.

Lesson outline (for the teacher's and students' notebooks):

1. Hezekiah's sickness and healing (2 Kings 20:1-11; Isaiah 38:1-8; 2 Chronicles 32:25).
2. Hezekiah's pride and punishment (2 Kings 20:12-19; Isaiah 39:1-8; 2 Chronicles 32:25-33).
3. Manasseh's pride and punishment (2 Kings 21:1-16; 2 Chronicles 33:1-24).
4. Assyria's pride and punishment (Nahum 1:1-3:19).

The verse to be memorized:

If My people, which are called by My name, shall humble themselves, and pray, and seek My face, and turn from their wicked ways, then will I hear from Heaven, and will forgive their sin, and will heal their land.

(2 Chronicles 7:14)

NOTE TO THE TEACHER

Mrs. Charles Hufstetler who served on our Editorial Board, had a life-time of missionary service in the Philippines. She wrote: "Many believers think of prayer as only 'asking' or maybe tacking on a 'thank you.' The simple outline (appearing before point 3 of the lesson), helped our new believers and children to pray Biblically. Praying this way keeps the focus on God rather than us. Praying together after the lesson stamps it on the students' minds."

THE LESSON
1. KING HEZEKIAH'S SICKNESS AND HEALING
2 Kings 20:1-11; Isaiah 38:1-8; 2 Chronicles 32:25

Good King Hezekiah became very, very sick. **ISAIAH**, God's **prophet**, went to see him. **ISAIAH** spoke seriously. "King Hezekiah, the Lord says you are going to die. Do you have anything to take care of before dying? If so, do it now." Having said this, **ISAIAH** walked out.

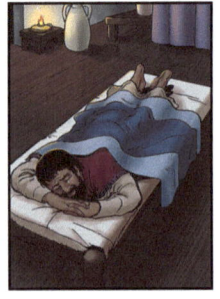

Show Illustration #5

King Hezekiah was terrified. Turning his face to the wall, he did what he usually did. What was that? (*He prayed*.) Crying, Hezekiah prayed, "O Lord, remember that I have walked before You truthfully with a perfect heart. I have done what is good in Your sight."

Then God immediately spoke to **ISAIAH** saying, "Go back to Hezekiah. Tell him I have seen his tears and heard his prayer. Tell him I shall heal him. Three (3) days from now he will be strong–well enough to go to My temple. He will live another 15 years. And here is what I shall do to prove this will come true: on the sun dial I shall cause the shadow of the sun to go backward ten degrees."

ISAIAH hurried to deliver this good news to King Hezekiah. And exactly what God said would happen, did happen. (See Isaiah 38:4-8.) The sun's shadow moved backward instead of forward. (*Teacher:* If possible, show a sun dial. Let students see what it meant for the sun's shadow to go backward.) It was a miracle! And, like all miracles, it cannot be explained. God did this miracle just for King Hezekiah. And King Hezekiah was healed of his sickness. Do you think

Hezekiah was thankful to the Lord for answering his prayer? (See Isaiah 38:16-19.) Of course he was! But at the same time, he felt proud and puffed up. (See 2 Chronicles 32:25.) Did you hear that? Good King Hezekiah was proud! He thought he was someone special because God answered his prayer. Do you ever feel proud when God answers your prayers?

2. HEZEKIAH'S PRIDE AND PUNISHMENT
2 Kings 20:12-19; Isaiah 39:1-8; 2 Chronicles 32:25-33

Far, far from Judah, the king of Babylon (use back cover map) heard about King Hezekiah's sickness. He learned, too, that God had healed Hezekiah. More than this, Babylon's king knew about the sun's shadow going backward. It sounded like magic to him! The king of Babylon was not interested in the true and living God of Heaven. But he wanted to know about the shadow of the sun going backward. (See 2 Chronicles 32:31.) So he sent his messengers with letters and a present for King Hezekiah.

The king and people of Babylon did not love the living God. They were idol worshipers. Yet when the king's men came to Godly King Hezekiah, he was delighted. Now you should know something which even King Hezekiah did not know. The Lord allowed these men to come so He could test Hezekiah. The test would show what was in King Hezekiah's heart. (See 2 Chronicles 32:3 1.)

Show Illustration #6

King Hezekiah welcomed the king's men from Babylon. Proudly he showed them the palace and his stacks and stacks of gold and silver. He showed off the swords and spears lining the walls. He wanted to prove how great and important he was. The nien of Babylon saw absolutely everything in King Hezekiah's kingdom! (See **Isaiah** 39:2.) Hezekiah acted as if these great riches were his. He seemed to have forgotten that God had given him everything.

Immediately after the men from Babylon left, the prophet **ISAIAH** came to Hezekiah. **ISAIAH** asked, "Where did those men come from?"

Hezekiah answered, "They came from faraway Babylon."

ISAIAH wanted to know, "What did they see here?"

Hezekiah answered proudly, "I showed them everything in my palace and all my treasures everywhere."

ISAIAH exclaimed, "Listen to what God says: 'The time will come when everything in your palace and all your riches will be taken to Babylon! Nothing will be left! Even your family will be taken. They will become servants in the palace of the king of Babylon.'"

King Hezekiah could hardly believe what he had heard. All his money, his treasures, and his family would be taken to Babylon. And it was his own fault. God had tested him, and he proved he was proud. His pride had caused him to act foolishly.

Pride is a sin God hates. (See Proverbs 6:16-17; 8:13; 16:5, 18; 29:23; 1 John 2:16.) Always remember that everything you can do, and all you have, comes from God. In a flash, He could take away every ability and everything you have.

Do you get puffed up when someone says something nice about you? Do you feel you are special because of what you have? Do you boast when you do something well? Do you think you are better than others? Do you show off to get attention? Whatever makes you feel above others, is pride. And pride, like all sin, must be confessed to God. (See Proverbs 28:13; 1 John 1:9.) Otherwise the Lord may severely punish you.

(*Teacher:* Allow time for students to confess silently any known pride.)

3. MANASSEH'S PRIDE AND PUNISHMENT
2 Kings 21:1-16; 2 Chronicles 33:1-24

Probably everyone has something better or can do something better than someone else. This is not wrong. It is sinful when we become proud of what we have or do. King Hezekiah had been a good man, a man who prayed about everything. But he was proud and showed off his treasures. So God said the treasures would be taken to Babylon. And, later, they were. (See Daniel 1:1-3.)

The time came when King Hezekiah died. And his son, Manasseh, became king. King Manasseh was entirely different from his father. He was so wicked, it is hard to imagine he was Hezekiah's son.

Manasseh built idols to false gods all through the land of Judah. He placed in God's holy temple a carved idol which he had made. (See 2 Chronicles 33:7.) He even sacrificed his children to false gods! (See 2 Chronicles 33:6.) He practiced witchcraft and all kinds of terrible wickedness. Instead of worshiping God, he worshiped the sun, moon, and stars which God created. And King Manasseh led the people of Judah and Jerusalem away from God. They even became worse than the heathen nations God had destroyed. (See 2 Chronicles 33:9-10.)

So the Lord sent prophets to Manasseh and the people of Judah. One prophet said, "King Manasseh has done more evil than those before him. With his idols he has made Judah sin. Because of this, the Lord God says: 'I shall bring evil upon Jerusalem and Judah. I shall punish Jerusalem. I shall wipe it away. I shall hand My people over to their enemies. They have done evil and made Me angry' . . ." (See 2 Kings 21:1-15.)

But Manasseh and the people of Judah were proud. They would not listen to God nor His prophets. (See 2 Chronicles 33:10.)

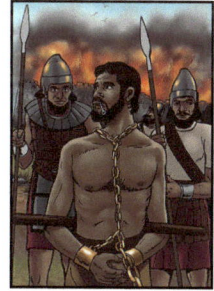

Show Illustration #7

So God sent the cruel Assyrian army into Jerusalem. The commanders captured King Manasseh. They pierced a hook in his nose and bound him with chains. Then they led him away like a bull to a far-off prison in Babylon. (See 2 Chronicles 33:11.)

There King Manasseh had much time to think. Did he think of his father, good King Hezekiah? Did he contrast his own ungodly life with his father's Godly life? Did he know the words of our verse? (Have students quote 2 Chronicles 7:14.)

In prison, Manasseh had many thoughts. He remembered how self-important he felt when he chose not to worship God. Proudly he had turned (and led his people to turn) to idols. Together they worshiped their manmade gods. Manasseh thought of his stubbornness in refusing to listen to God's prophets. He refused to believe their warnings. So God allowed him to be captured and chained by the Assyrians. How humiliated he was to be led away with a hook in his nose! He had gone from the palace in Jerusalem to prison in Babylon. (Show on map.)

Perhaps there he remembered the words of the great King Solomon: "When pride comes, then comes shame. But with the lowly [humble] comes wisdom." (See Proverbs 11:2.) "A man's pride shall bring him low. But honor shall uphold the humble in spirit" (Proverbs 29:23).

Finally, Manasseh "humbled himself greatly before the Lord God and prayed to Him." (See 2 Chronicles 33:12.)

Would God hear the prayer of one who had been so wicked? (*Teacher:* Encourage discussion.)

God did hear Manasseh's prayer and forgave his sin. He even took the king back to Jerusalem and his kingdom. Then King Manasseh knew that the Lord is God. (See 2 Chronicles 33:12-13.) God humbles those who are proud. And "he who humbles himself shall be exalted." (The words of the Lord Jesus in Matthew 23:12.)

Back in his own land, Manasseh was a different man. He got rid of the man-made gods. He took from God's temple the carved idol he had made. He destroyed the idol altars he had built on the temple hill and in Jerusalem. He repaired God's altar. Then he sacrificed offerings to the Lord. He commanded the people of Judah, saying, "Serve the Lord your God." And many obeyed him and turned back to the Lord. (See 2 Chronicles 33:17.)

4. ASSYRIA'S PRIDE AND PUNISHMENT
Nahum 1:1-3:19

The people of judah were glad to have King Manasseh home. Now that he had turned to God, he was entirely different. Yet when they saw him, they were reminded of the powerful Assyrians. They remembered how proudly the Assyrians had led away their king like a bull.

The people of Judah wondered if the Israelites were being tortured in Assyria. Many cruel Assyrians were neighbors now. They were living right next to Judah in what had been Israel's homeland. So the people of Judah were afraid.

Because God knew their fears, He sent His **prophet NAHUM** to Judah. **NAHUM** tried at once to calm the people by speaking of God Himself. He said, "The Lord is jealous of those He loves. [He certainly did love the people of Judah.] God is against His enemies. [Judah's enemies, the Assyrians, were also God's enemies.] The Lord is slow to anger. He has great power. [God has even more power than the powerful Assyrians!] The Lord is good, a refuge in times of trouble. He cares for those who trust in Him." (See Nahum 1:2-3, 7.)

NAHUM wanted God's people to know that God always controls everything. So he told them what God would do some day to Nineveh, Assyria's capital. "God says, 'I shall destroy the carved images and the idols which are in the temple of their gods. (See **Nahum** 1:14.) With an overrunning flood I shall make an end of Nineveh. The place will collapse. Nineveh will be like a pool." (See **Nahum** 1:8; 2:6, 8.)

The Assyrians had become very rich by stealing from those whom they captured. So **NAHUM** gave God's warning: "A day will come when Nineveh's enemies will rob their silver and gold. All their treasures will be taken. (See **Nahum** 2:9.) Their enemies will ride into their city in horse-drawn chariots. With their flashing swords and shining spears they will kill Nineveh's people. There will be piles of dead, more bodies than can be counted!" (See **Nahum** 3:2-3.)

Show Illustration #8

NAHUM continued his prophecy from God. "Enemy soldiers will enter Nineveh. They will set fire to the barred city gates. (See **Nahum** 3:13.) The city will be burned down. (See **Nahum** 3:15.) The city officers will run away and hide. (See **Nahum** 3:17.) No one will be left in Nineveh. They will have no descendants. Because your people are vile, I shall bury them," God declared. (See **Nahum** 1:14.)

NAHUM ended his prophecy with these sad words from God: "O Assyria, your leaders will die. Your people will be scattered. No one will gather them. Nineveh will be in such ruins it will never be rebuilt. And all who hear the report of its destruction, will clap their hands. Why? Because you have been cruel to them." (See **Nahum** 3:18-19.) Proud Assyria's capital city, Nineveh, would be gone forever.

Assyria was so powerful it was not easy to believe **NAHUM**'s prophecy. But you must hear this: Absolutely everything God said, came true. *Everything*! Even to this day, Nineveh has never been rebuilt. God hates pride and He punishes nations and people who are proud. What are you proud about? Will you confess it to God right now? (*Teacher:* You may have to mention kinds of pride which could affect your students. Allow time for them to talk to God silently.)

Pride is one sin which takes hold of us in surprising ways. At the close of each day look into your own heart. Have you been boastful? Have you felt more important than others? Have you been a show-off? Confess each proud act and ask God's forgiveness.

Write in your notebook these Scripture references and keep them before you always.

> Romans 12:3–We are not to think of ourselves more highly than we ought.
>
> James 4:6–God resists the proud but gives grace to the humble.
>
> 1 Peter 5:6–Humble yourselves under God's mighty hand.

To be humble is to be modest, yielding, mild, gentle, unshowy, not boastful, not self-important. God wants you to be a truly humble Christian.

Lesson 3
GOD'S WORD IS POWERFUL

Scripture to be studied: 2 Kings 22:1-23:30; 2 Chronicles 34:1-35:26; Zephaniah 1:1-3:20

The *aim* of the lesson: To teach the power of God's Word and the importance of God-like living.

What your students should *know*: Josiah obeyed God's Word. His Godly living helped the people of Judah.

> **NOTE TO THE TEACHER**
>
> Two words in the lesson outline should be made clear to your students.
> 1. *Condemn* means to announce a person is guilty of sin.
> 2. *Convict* means that the person is proved guilty.
>
> The prophet ZEPHANIAH featured in this lesson, came from a royal family. His great-great grandfather was King Hezekiah. King Josiah (of whom we learn in this lesson was King Hezekiah's great grandson. Therefore these tow men were distantly related. This could account for King Josiah's particular interest in ZEPHANIAH's prophecy.

What your students should *feel*: A desire to live a God-like life which will help others to turn to God.

What your students should *do*: Read and obey the Word of God so their lives will cause others to live for Him.

Lesson outline (for the teacher's and students' notebooks):
1. God's Word condemns (Zephaniah 1:1-3:20).
2. God's Word convicts (2 Kings 22:8-14; 2 Chronicles 34:3-21).
3. God's Word teaches (2 Kings 22:15-20; 2 Chronicles 34:22-28).
4. God's Word guides (2 Kings 23:1-25; 2 Chronicles 34:29-35:19).

The verse to be memorized:

> *If My people, which are called by My name, shall humble themselves, and pray, and seek My face, and turn from their wicked ways, then will I hear from Heaven, and will forgive their sin, and will heal their land.*
>
> (2 Chronicles 7:14)

THE LESSON

When wicked Manasseh humbled himself and turned to God, God forgave him. Imniediately Manasseh did what he could to help his people turn back to God. But many continued living wickedly as Manasseh had led them. His wicked son (Amon), Judah's next king, reigned two years. Then his people killed him and made his son, Josiah, king.

King Josiah was only eight years old and he had much to learn. But right from the beginning, he did what was pleasing to God. When he was 16 years old, he purposed to live a Godly life. (See 2 Kings 22:2; 2 Chronicles 34:1-3.)

At about this time, God sent to Jerusalem one of his **prophets**, ZEPHANIAH. When ZEPHANIAH spoke, King Josiah would listen.

1. GOD'S WORD CONDEMNS
Zephaniah 1:1-3:20

Show Illustration #9

ZEPHANIAH began, "The Lord says, 'I shall sweep away everything from the face of the earth. I shall sweep away men, animals, birds, and fish . . . I shall cut off man from the face of the earth. I shall stretch out My hand against Judah and all who live in Jerusalem." (See **Zephaniah** 1:1-4.) King Josiah understood that God would destroy His disobedient people.

God reminded His people that He was against idol worshipers. He also would punish those who worshiped the sun, moon, and stars (as King Manasseh had done, 2 Kings 21:3). God would punish those who turned away from Him, those who did not seek Him. (See **Zephaniah** 1:4b-6.) God's powerful words through ZEPHANIAH condemned God's people. But God always loves His people. So He pled with them, saying, "Seek the Lord, all you who arc humble. Obey His commands. Seek to do right." (See **Zephaniah** 2:3.)

Would God punish His own people only? Oh, no! Through ZEPHANIAH, God said He would punish those in neighboring lands (use back cover map): Philistia, Moab, Ammon, Cush (Ethiopia), Assyria. (See **Zephaniah** 2:4-15.) To His own people in Judah, God made this wonderful promise: Philistia, Moab, and Ammon would some day belong to them. (See **Zephaniah** 2:7, 9b.) But He would totally destroy Assyria. Its capital city, Nineveh, would be empty "and dry as the desert." (See **Zephaniah** 2:13.) God would never forget their wicked cruelty. He, the powerful One, condemns those who sin.

God spoke finally (through ZEPHANIAH) of a day which has not yet come. God said, "In that day, My people will not be proud. They will do no wrong. They will neither lie nor be deceitful. (See **Zephaniah** 3:11-13.) The Lord [Christ], the king of Israel, will be with you (**Zephaniah** 3:15). In that day, you will have nothing to fear. I shall punish your enemies and bring you back to your homeland. (See **Zephaniah** 3:19-20.) I shall give you honor and praise among all people of the earth. This will happen before your very eyes!"

2. GOD'S WORD CONVICTS
2 Kings 22:8-14; 2 Chronicles 34:3-21

King Josiah was delighted that God's people would some day have a wonderful future. But what about those who were idol worshipers? Unless they turned to God, God would destroy them.

By the time King Josiah was age 20, he knew what he had to do. He announced: "The idols and heathen altars must be destroyed. Come with me. We shall break them to pieces." The king and his men traveled throughout the whole land. They broke down all the idols, the images, the altars to false gods.

— 25 —

They smashed them and crushed them into powder. This took a long time.

Now King Josiah was 26 years old. So he commanded, "The temple must be restored. We have been collecting money to do this. Hire carpenters and masons. Get as many workers as you need to repair God's house. Pay those who do the work."

Many, many years before, King Hezekiah's men had repaired the temple. But afterwards, wicked King Manasseh killed God's true priests and temple workers. So for years, God's temple had been ignored. Now, much would have to be done so it could be used again. King Josiah's men went right to work–and they worked faithfully! (See 2 Chronicles 34:12.)

While they were cleaning inside the temple, a priest (Hilkiah) found a book. In those days, books were written on scrolls. He hurried to Shaphan, the man in charge. "Look what I found!" he exclaimed. "It is the book of God's Law."

Show Illustration #10

Shaphan took God's Law book in his hands. In it were the laws God had given through Moses. (The books of Genesis, Exodus, Leviticus, Numbers, Deuteronomy.) What a find! Shaphan's hands trembled as he held God's Law. "I wonder how long it has been lost," Shaphan murmured. Then he exclaimed, "The king must see this at once!" And he rushed to the king.

"O King Josiah," Shaphan began, "the priest found God's Law book. He brought it to me. I shall read it to you." And Shaphan read God's Word to King Josiah. What part of God's word did he read? We do not know. He could have read that the king was to make a copy of God's Law. And the king was to read it. By reading it, he would know how to do God's will. (See Deuteronomy 17:18-19.) Shaphan may have read these words of God, "When My people turn away from Me, I shall send a strong enemy nation to destroy them." (See Deuteronomy 28:45-50.) Whatever Shaphan read, the king was terrified.

"We have disobeyed God and His Law!" King Josiah exclaimed. Then he tore his robes, showing his great sadness. He cried, "The Lord's anger burns against us. Our fathers have not done what His law says." God's powerful Word had convicted the king.

The prophet **ZEPHANIAH** had announced God's people were guilty. They were condemned. God's Word, written on the scroll, proved they were guilty. They were convicted.

Like the people of Josiah's day, we too choose to go our own way. (See Isaiah 53:6.) Going our own way instead of God's way, is sin. So we are guilty of sin. God placed on the Lord Jesus Christ the sin of all of us. He died on the cross taking our punishment for sin. When we believe in the Lord Jesus and receive Him as our Saviour, He forgives our sin. And He gives us everlasting life. (See John 3:16, 36; 5:24.)

The Lord Jesus is waiting to receive you. Will you receive Him today? (*Teacher:* Expand invitation as needed for your group.)

3. GOD'S WORD TEACHES
2 Kings 22:15-20; 2 Chronicles 34:22-28

King Josiah was convicted by God's powerful Word written on the scroll.

Turning to the priest and some other men, King Josiah gave orders. "Go to the **prophetess HULDAH**. (**HULDAH** was a lady prophet.) "Ask her what God says, and what we should do," Josiah commanded.

Show Illustration #11

The men hurried to **HULDAH**, the prophetess. She told them, "Tell King Josiah the Lord God says this: 'What the king has read (in God's Law), I [God] shall do. My people have turned away from Me. They have worshiped idols. So I am angry with them and shall severely punish them.' Also tell the king, 'Because you, Josiah, humbled yourself–you tore your robes and wept–I have heard you. I shall punish My people. But I shall not punish them until after you die. You will not see the disaster I shall bring to this place." God knew that King Josiah had lived a Godly life. He was truly sorry for the sins of the people. Because this was so, Josiah would not be punished.

The king's men were glad to tell him, "God's punishment will not come while you are living!"

God is a wonderful Teacher. He speaks to His own and teaches them His ways.

4. GOD'S WORD GUIDES
2 Kings 23:1-25; 2 Chronicles 34:29-35:19

King Josiah called together all the people of Jerusalem. Everyone came: leaders, fathers, mothers, children, everyone. Standing by the pillar of the temple, King Josiah read God's Law to them. He promised to follow the Lord and obey His commands. He would do this, he said, with all "his heart and soul." He would obey the words "written in this Book" (2 Chronicles 34:31). All the people made the same promise along with their king. And, "as long as Josiah lived, they did not fail to follow the Lord." (See 2 Chronicles 34:33.) King Josiah was a good example and his people followed him.

Show Illustration #12

King Josiah learned there were still more idols to be destroyed. He took care of that, you may be sure. He even sent to Bethel (in Israel) and smashed the altar of the calf idol! (See 2 Kings 23:15.)

Then he ordered the people, "Come, celebrate the Passover as it is written in God's Law." Hundreds and hundreds gathered at God's temple. They perfectly followed God's instruction about the Passover. Josiah commanded, "Kill the Passover lambs. Set yourselves apart for God. Do what the Lord commanded Moses." And everyone obeyed.

At the time of the very first Passover, God had said, "When I see the blood (on the top and sides of the doorpost) I shall pass over you." (See Exodus 12:1-14.) Each lamb died in place of the oldest son in the family. From then on, one perfect lamb died for the sins of each family. So King Josiah and his people celebrated Passover the same way.

Since the Lord Jesus Christ died, we no longer celebrate Passover. He is the perfect Lamb of God who sacrificed Himself once for all. (See 1 Corinthians 5:7; Hebrews 9:12.) When He died on the cross, He took our sins on Himself. (See 1 Peter 2:24.) If we truly trust Him as our Saviour, God forgives our sin.

King Josiah was a good king. He knew God's Word and obeyed it. He was a splendid leader who was led by God's

Word. How did Josiah lead his people? (*Teacher:* Question your students on the following.)

1. What did he destroy? (*The idols, images, the altars to false gods*)
2. What did he read? (*God's Word*)
3. What did he learn from the prophetess? (*The meaning of God's Word. We, too, should listen to those who can teach us the meaning of God's Word.*)
4. With whom did King Josiah share what he learned from God's Word? (*God's people*)
5. With all his people around hini, what did King Josiah promise? (*He promised to obey God's Word.*)
6. Did he obey God's Word? (*Yes!*)
7. Did he lead his people to worship God? (*He surely did.*)
8. In the words of our verse, what could King Josiah have told God's people? (*God says: "If My people, who are called by My name, shall humble themselves, and pray, and seek My face, and turn from their nicked nays, then nil! I hear from Heaven, and will forgive their sin and will heal their land. (2 Chronicles 7:14.)*)

King Josiah followed the teachings of God's Word. No other king before or after Josiah, followed God's Law more carefully than he. Do you faithfully read and obey God's Word? Is your life a good example to others?

What would God lead you to do if you read this in His Word: "Be ye kind one to another . . . forgiving one another, even as God, for Christ's sake, has forgiven you"? (Ephesians 4:32.) To whom would you be kind? Whom would you forgive?

(*Teacher:* If your students are married, have them read Ephesians 5:22-33; Colossians 3:18-19. For those who drink wine, use Ephesians 5:18. For children, use Ephesians 6:1-3. For those who are employed, Ephesians 6:5-7; Colossians 3:22-24. For employers, Ephesians 6:9; Colossians 4:1. For all, Colossians 3:9, 12-13, 16; Philippians 4:6, 8.)

When we read God's Word, He may condemn us, declaring we are guilty of sin. He may convict us, so that we know we are guilty. But He will teach us so we shall know to do right. And He will guide us. Make certain you read God's Word every day. Then He can speak to you. Think about what He says and obey Him. Then you can live a Godly life.

Lesson 4
GOD PUNISHES DISOBEDIENCE

NOTE TO THE TEACHER

From the beginning, God hated idolatry. When He gave His Law to the Israelites, he warned them against idol-worship. (See Exodus 20:3-5.) Just before they entered the land God gave them, He again warned them. (See, for examaple, Deuteronomy 27:15.) At the same time, He promised them blessings for obedience would result in terrible punishment. God foretold the exact punishment 700 years beforehand! (See Deuteronomy 28:49-57.) That punishment finally came, as we shall see in this lesson.

This concludes our study of 1 and 2 Kings, 1 and 2 Chronicles, and nine of the Minor Prophets. The people of Israel had been captured by the Assyrians. Now (136 years later) the people of Judah are carried away, prisoners of Babylon. So the nation of Israel (which had been torn apart into the Northern and Southern Kingdoms) is now torn from their land.

Before the beginning your study, read the sad words of 2 Chronicles 36:14-20. Observe that it was God Himself who handed His people over to Babylon. After you have prepared the lesson, read 2 Chronicles 36:22-23. God remembered His people then. Today, more than 3,000 years later, He still remembers them. The best is yet ahead for Israel, whom God chose for Himself! (See Ezekiel 37:21-28.) Wonderful, wonderful Lord!

Scripture to be studied: 2 Kings 23:29-24:21; 2 Chronicles 35:20-36:21; Jeremiah 25:1-9; 36:1-31; Habakkuk 1:1-3:19; Luke 1:31-33

The *aim* of the lesson: To teach the seriousness of ignoring God's warnings.

What your students should *know*: God always keeps His word. He punishes disobedience; He blesses obedience.

What your students should *feel*: A desire to know and obey God's warnings.

What your students should *do*: Pay attention to the warnings in God's Word; repent if they have ignored His Word.

Lesson outline (for the teacher's and students' notebooks):

1. Judah loses God's king (2 Kings 23:29-24:7; 2 Chronicles 35:20-36:7).
2. Judah hears God's warnings (2 Chronicles 36:1-23; Jeremiah 25:1-11; 36:1-23; Habakkuk 1:1-2:20).
3. Judah suffers God's punishment (2 Kings 23:34-25:21; 2 Chronicles 36:5-21).
4. Judah has God's promises (2 Samuel 7:11b-16; 1 Kings 11:9-13; 15:4; 2 Chronicles 21:6-7; Luke 1:31-33).

The verse to be memorized:

If My people, which are called by My name, shall humble themselves, and pray, and seek My face, and turn from their wicked ways, then will I hear from Heaven, and will forgive their sin, and will heal their land.

(2 Chronicles 7:14)

THE LESSON

Suppose someone told you, "I am promising you this." Would you expect something good or bad? (Encourage student response.) If someone said, "I am warning you!" What would you expect?

A promise is usually something good to look forward to. A warning tells of something bad which will happen. God has given both promises and warnings in His Word. He warned He would punish His people for turning from Him to idols. At the same time, God made a promise to King Josiah. He said, "The punishment will not conic while you live."

1. JUDAH LOSES GOD'S KING
2 Kings 23:29-24:7; 2 Chronicles 35:20-36:7

The nations surrounding King Josiah in Judah had great armies. The king of Egypt was marching his army through Judah to Assyria. (Show back cover map.) There the Egyptians would join the Assyrians. Together their armies would fight against powerful Babylon. But King Josiah did not want the Egyptians in his land. So he led his army against the Egyptians. As they fought, an arrow struck King Josiah. He cried, "Take me away! I'm wounded!"

Show Illustration #13

His men laid him in another chariot and rushed him to Jerusalem. That night, good King Josiah lay dead. Judah's king was gone. There had never been such a good king before or after Josiah. He lived a very Godly life. He had turned to the Lord with all his heart, soul, and strength. And he truly obeyed the Law of God. (See 2 Kings 23:15.)

God had promised not to punish Judah while Josiah lived. But now King Josiah was dead and Egypt took control of Judah.

Josiah's son (Jehoahaz)–an evil, ungodly man–was the next king of Judah. In only three months, the Egyptian king took away his crown. He bound Judah's king in chains, making him a prisoner of Egypt.

2. JUDAH HEARS GOD'S WARNINGS
2 Chronicles 36:1-23; Jeremiah 25:1-11; 36:1-23; Habakkuk 1:1-2:20

Immediately the Egyptian king placed another wicked king on Judah's throne. He re-named him Jehoiakim.

At this time, God sent the **JEREMIAH** to His people. **JEREMIAH** began, "For 23 years I have warned you again and again. But you have not listened. Other prophets also warned you, saying, 'Turn from your evil ways. If you do, you can stay forever in this land God gave you. Do not follow other gods.' But you have not listened. Now God says this to you: 'You have not obeyed Me. So I shall cause the king of Babylon to destroy Judah. I shall make Judah a desolate wasteland. And you will serve the king of Babylon 70 years'." (See **Jeremiah** 25:1-11.)

Did you hear that? God's people were already controlled by Egypt. Now God said they would be captives of Babylon–for 70 years! Would God's people ever listen to His warnings? Do *you* listen when God warns you?

A day came when God told **JEREMIAH**: "On a scroll write My warnings to Judah. Tell them everything I have told you since the time of King Josiah. Again My people will learn about the terrible punishment I shall bring upon them. Perhaps then they will turn from their wicked ways. If thee do, I shall forgive them." (See **Jeremiah** 36:1-3.)

Show Illustration #14

JEREMIAH immediately called his assistant, Baruch. "Write on a scroll God's message," **JEREMIAH** said. Baruch wrote quickly everything **JEREMIAH** told him. There, in writing, were all God's warnings of punishment. The wonderful promise of God's forgiveness was also on the scroll. God really wanted His people to turn to Him so He could forgive them.

When everything was written on the scroll, **JEREMIAH** told Baruch, "Take God's message to the temple. From the scroll, read God's word to the people. Perhaps those who hear will turn from their wickedness to the Lord." (See **Jeremiah** 36:4-7.)

Baruch hurried to obey **JEREMIAH**. At the temple, the people listened to God's warnings. One man ran to the palace telling what he had heard. The king's men commanded, "Get the scroll and bring it here!" One whispered to Baruch, "You and **JEREMIAH** go and hide. Do not let anyone know where you are!" (See **Jeremiah** 36:8-19.)

Soon one of the king's men read the scroll to King Jehoiakim. Keeping warm by the fire, the king listened, and became wild with rage! (See **Jeremiah** 36:20-22.)

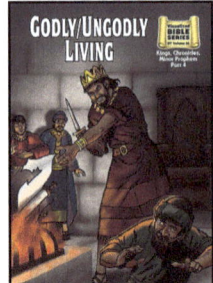

Show Front Cover

He grabbed the scroll, slashed it in pieces, and pitched it into the fire. His men coaxed him not to burn it. But the king refused to listen. (See **Jeremiah** 36:23, 25.) So all God's warnings and promises were burned to ashes.

King Jehoiakim brushed his hands, glad to be rid of God's words. He had no fear of God's warning of punishment. He did not tear his clothes, showing sorrow for sin. God's words meant nothing to him. (**Jeremiah** 36:24.)

King Jehoiakim commanded his men: "Arrest Baruch and **JEREMIAH**!" But neither man could be found, for the Lord had hidden them! (See **Jeremiah** 36:26.)

Were God's words really gone? God told **JEREMIAH**, "Get another scroll. Write down all that was on the first scroll. And I shall tell you even more. Put it all in writing." (**Jeremiah** 36:27-28, 32.)

JEREMIAH obeyed. Then God said, "Tell King Jehoiakim this: Because he destroyed God's words, I shall punish him. None of his sons will sit on the throne of David. (See **Jeremiah** 36:30-31.) When he dies, his body will be thrown on the garbage heap." For destroying God's precious Word, this would be Jehoiakim's awful punishment. God's Word is always to be handled carefully and lovingly.

Another prophet, **HABAKKUK**, was in Judah at this time. Prophets usually took God's messages to His people. But **HABAKKUK** took questions to God. He asked, "Why are You, O God, allowing so much wickedness?" (See **Habakkuk** 1:2-4.)

God answered, "Wait until you see what I am going to do. I shall use the Babylonians [sometimes called Chaldeans] to sweep across the earth. They will conquer everyone–including My people. They have a god–it is their strength." (See **Habakkuk** 1:5-11.)

HABAKKUK said, "O Lord, You are everlasting. You are holy. We are wicked. But the Babylonians are even more wicked. Why are You, the Holy One, using them to punish us? We are as helpless as fish. They will catch us with hooks and scoop us into their nets." (See **Habakkuk** 1:12-17.)

God answered, "Write on tablets what I tell you. Those who read My message can run and tell the news throughout the land." On tablets, **HABAKKUK** wrote these words from God: "The Babylonians are proud and trust in themselves. People who are righteous trust in Me and live. I [God] shall severely punish those who are greedy (2:6-8); the selfish; and those who get rich by evil means (2:9-11). I shall punish those who are cruel to their workmen (2:12-14); drunkards (2:15-17); idol worshipers" (2:18-19).

God closed His message saying, "The Lord is in His holy temple. Let all the earth be silent before Him" (**Habakkuk** 2:20). God was reminding His people that He controls everything.

God's messages were usually spoken by His prophets. Now **HABAKKUK** had God's words written on tablets. And **JEREMIAH** had God's words on a scroll. So the people throughout Judah could read God's warnings.

There are no prophets today to tell us God's messages. God's words are not written on tablets or scrolls. God's Word is printed now in our Bible. In it, we have everything He wants us to know. Every day we can read His promises and warnings. The Bible teaches us how to live Godly lives. By obeying God's Word, we are kept from living ungodly lives.

Some people laugh at the Bible, for they think it is untrue. Some hate the Bible and, like Jehoiakim, have tried to destroy it. But the Bible is God's Word. And He has His ways of keeping it safe.

Do you love to read the Bible? Do you take time to study it? Because it is God's Book, you will keep learning and learning His truths. And take good care of your Bible. Remember what happened to Jehoiakim who destroyed God's scroll!

3. JUDAH SUFFERS GOD'S PUNISHMENT
2 Kings 23:34-25:21; 2 Chronicles 36:5-21

The prophet **HABAKKUK** had asked God why He had allowed so much wickedness in Judah.

God told him, "Wait and see what I am going to do. I shall use the Babylonians to sweep across the earth. They will conquer everyone–including My people." In God's time, exactly as God had said, Babylon overtook Judah. The king of Babylon captured wicked King Jehoiakim. He bound Jehoiakim's legs and arms in chains and led him to Babylon. He also stole treasures from God's temple and took them to the temple of his gods.

Then Babylon's king chose another evil king for Judah. (See 2 Kings 24:8-16.) Soon he and 10,000 of Judah's best men were prisoners in Babylon. Only the poor and weak were left in Judah.

Judah's last king, Zedekiah, "hardened his heart and would not turn to the Lord" (2 Chronicles 36:13). And all God's people were as ungodly as their king. Even so, God pitied them and sent **messengers** to them. But they laughed at God's **messengers** and despised God's words. So God Himself handed His own dearly-loved people to Babylon's king. (See 2 Chronicles 36:11-19.) And this is how He did it:

God allowed the king of Babylon and his strong army to march to Jerusalem. They pitched camp around the city so no one could leave or enter. After two years there was no food in the city. The people were weak and hungry. So the king of Judah and his army escaped through a hole in the city wall. The army of Babylon raced after them and captured the king of Judah. And the rest of Judah's ragged army scattered.

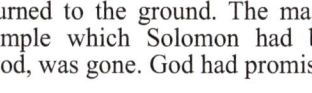

Show Illustration #15

Then the Babylonian commander marched right up to God's holy temple. He set fire to it and watched while it burned to the ground. The magnificent temple which Solomon had built for God, was gone. God had promised, "My name, My eyes, My heart will be there forever." (See 1 Kings 9:3.) But He had also warned, "If you [My people] turn from following Me and disobey Me by worshiping other gods–then I shall cut off My people out of the land. And this house I shall cast out of My sight." (See 1 Kings 9:6-7.)

Finally, many of God's people were dead. The rest were captured and taken to Babylon. The few leaders who were left were killed. And Jerusalem was totally destroyed. The people God had chosen for Himself were gone from the wonderful land He had chosen for them. And God allowed it because His people had turned away from Him. (See also 2 Kings 24:3-4.) They chose to live ungodly lives.

4. JUDAH HAS GOD'S PROMISES
2 Samuel 7:11-16; 1 Kings 11:9-13; 15:4; 2 Chronicles 21:6-7; Luke 1:31-33

Was this the end of God's people? Were the kingdom and temple gone forever? No! In the promises of God, there were some "forevers." And forever means time without end. God had promised Abraham a nation and a land forever (Genesis 13:14-17). He promised David a kingdom forever (2 Samuel 7:13, 16). He spoke to Solomon of a temple forever (1 Kings 9:3).

Will the promised kingdom continue? Listen to this from God's Word: ". . . The children of Israel shall abide many days [a long, long time] without a king . . . *Afterward* the children of Israel shall return and seek their God and David their king. They shall come with fear to the Lord God and to His goodness in the latter days" (see Hosea 3:4-5). (This promise has not yet come true.)

A few hundred years later God gave another promise. It is in the New Testament. An angel spoke God's message to Mary who was from King David's family. "Fear not, Mary, for you have found favor with God. You shall have a Son and call His name JESUS. He shall be great, and shall be called the Son of the highest. The Lord God shall give Him the throne of His father David. And He shall reign over the house of Jacob (which includes Israel and Judah). Of His kingdom there shall be no end" (Luke 1:31-33).

Part of this promise came true months later. The Lord Jesus was born. The rest of God's promise has not come true even yet. Christ is not on a throne in Jerusalem. He could have reigned while He was here on earth. But the people of Israel refused to have Christ as their King. They shouted, "Crucify Him! Crucify Him!" And He died praying for them, "Father, forgive them, for they know not what they do." He died for their sins and for ours. (See Acts 10:43.) Christ died, but He arose and lives now in Heaven with God.

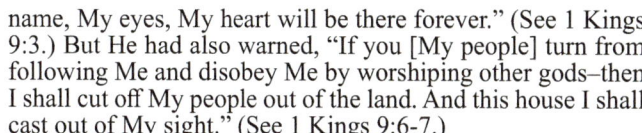

Show Illustration #16

In God's time, the Lord Jesus Christ from David's family, will return to earth. Then (like all God's other promises) the rest of the angel's promise will come true. Christ, the King, will sit on a throne in Jerusalem. There He will reign for 1,000 years and then in Heaven forever.

Until then, He is waiting for people everywhere to turn to Him. Those who refuse Him, will be punished forever and ever. If you have never received the Lord Jesus as your Saviour, will you do so right now?

(*Teacher:* Encourage students who want to come to Christ to talk with you after class.)

NOTE TO THE TEACHER

For the most part, this *Visualized Bible Series* follows the Biblical order of the books. However, Old Testament Volumes 24, 25, and 26 are taught chronologically. Examine the excellent charts below. Immediately you will understand the importance of including the nine Minor Prophets in these volumes,

THE ORDER OF EVENTS IN THE BOOKS OF THE OLD TESTAMENT

The arrangement of the books of the Old Testament does not follow the chronological order in which the recorded events occurred. The following listing shows which books cover approximately the same periods of time.

Genesis and Job
Exodus and Leviticus
Numbers and Deuteronomy
Joshua
Judges and Ruth
1 Samuel
2 Samuel and Psalms
1 King with 1 Chronicles, Song of Solomon, Proverbs, and Ecclesiastes
2 Kings with 2 Chronicles, Obadiah, Joel, Jonah, Amos, Hosea, Micah, Isaiah, Nahum, Zephaniah, Habakkuk, Jeremiah, and Lamentations
Daniel and Ezekiel
Ezra with Esther, Haggai, and Zechariah
Nehemiah and Malachi

www.ingramcontent.com/pod-product-compliance
Lightning Source LLC
Chambersburg PA
CBHW060800090426
42736CB00002B/100